Cool Healthy Muffins

Fun & Easy Baking Recipes for Kids!

Alex Kuskowski

Checkerboard Library

An Imprint of Abdo Publishing
www.abdopublishing.com

visit us at www.abdopublishing.com

Published by Abdo Publishing, a division of ABDO,
PO Box 398166, Minneapolis, Minnesota 55439. Copyright © 2015
by Abdo Consulting Group, Inc. International copyrights reserved
in all countries. No part of this book may be reproduced in any
form without written permission from the publisher. Checkerboard
Library™ is a trademark and logo of Abdo Publishing.

Printed in the United States of America, North Mankato, Minnesota
062014
092014

THIS BOOK CONTAINS
RECYCLED MATERIALS

Editor: Karen Latchana Kenney
Content Developer: Nancy Tuminelly
Cover and Interior Design and Production:
Colleen Dolphin, Mighty Media, Inc.
Food Production: Frankie Tuminelly
Photo Credits: Colleen Dolphin, Shutterstock

The following manufacturers/names appearing in this
book are trademarks: Bob's Red Mill®, Gold Medal®, Market Pantry®,
PAM®, Pillsbury®, Roundy's®

Library of Congress Cataloging-in-Publication Data
Kuskowski, Alex, author.
  Cool healthy muffins: fun & easy baking recipes for kids! /
Alex Kuskowski.
    pages cm. -- (Cool cupcakes & muffins)
  Audience: 8-12.
  Includes index.
  ISBN 978-1-62403-302-5
  1. Muffins--Juvenile literature. I. Title.
  TX770.M83K87 2015
  641.81'57--dc23
                    2013043081

To Adult Helpers

Assist a budding chef by
helping your child learn to cook.
Children develop new skills, gain
confidence, and make delicious
food when they cook. Some recipes
may be more difficult than others.
Offer help and guidance to your
child when needed. Encourage
creativity with recipes. Creative
cooking encourages children to
think like real chefs.

Before getting started, have ground
rules for using the kitchen, cooking
tools, and ingredients. There
should always be adult supervision
when a sharp tool, oven, or stove is
used. Be aware of the key symbols
described on page 9. They alert
you when certain things should be
monitored.

Put on your apron. Taste their
creations. Cheer on your new chef!

Contents

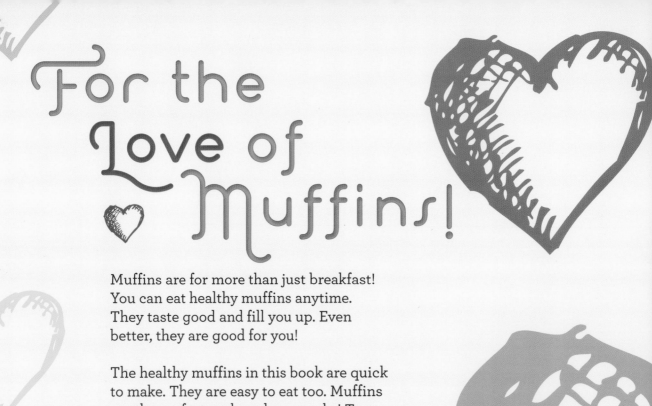

For the Love of ♡ Muffins!

Muffins are for more than just breakfast!
You can eat healthy muffins anytime.
They taste good and fill you up. Even
better, they are good for you!

The healthy muffins in this book are quick
to make. They are easy to eat too. Muffins
are the perfect grab-and-go snacks! Try
each of the recipes in this book. Or get
creative and make up your own!

This book has everything you need to get
started. It's filled with fun recipes. Follow
each recipe's easy steps to create tasty
treats. Get inspired to create muffins
that taste and look great!

The Basics

Ask Permission

Before you cook, ask **permission** to use the kitchen, cooking tools, and ingredients. If you'd like to do something yourself, say so! Just remember to be safe. If you would like help, ask for it! Always ask when you are using a stove or oven.

Be Prepared

→ Be organized. Knowing where everything is makes cooking safer and more fun!

→ Read the directions all the way through before starting the recipe. Remember to follow the directions in order.

→ The most important ingredient is preparation! Make sure you have everything you'll need.

Be Neat and Clean

→ Start with clean hands, clean tools, and a clean work surface.

→ Tie back long hair to keep it out of the food.

→ Wear comfortable clothing and roll up your sleeves.

→ Put on an apron if you have one. It'll keep your clothes clean.

Measuring

Many ingredients are measured by the cup, tablespoon, or teaspoon. Measuring tools may come in many sizes, but the amount they measure should be printed or **etched** on the sides of the tools. When measuring 1 cup, use the measuring cup marked 1 cup and fill it to the top.

Some ingredients are measured by weight in ounces or pounds. The weight is printed on the package label.

Be Smart, Be Safe

→ Never cook if you are home alone.

→ Always have an adult nearby for hot jobs, such as ones that use the oven or the stove.

→ Have an adult around when using a sharp tool, such as a knife or a **grater**. Always be careful when using these tools!

→ Remember to turn pot handles toward the back of the stove. That way you avoid accidentally knocking the pots over.

No Germs Allowed!

Raw eggs and raw meat have bacteria in them. These bacteria are killed when the food is cooked. But bacteria can survive on things the food touched and that can make you sick! After you handle raw eggs or meat, wash your hands, tools, and work surfaces with soap and water. Keep everything clean!

Cool Cooking Terms

Here are some basic cooking terms and actions that go with them. Whenever you need a reminder, just turn back to these pages.

Wash

Always wash fruits and vegetables well. Rinse them under cold water. Pat them dry with a **towel**. Then they won't slip when you cut them.

Dice

Dice means to cut something into small squares.

Grate

Grate means to shred something into small pieces using a **grater**.

Core

Core means to cut the middle out of something.

Symbols

Hot!

This recipe requires the use of a stove or oven. You will need adult **supervision** and assistance.

Sharp!

This recipe includes the use of a sharp **utensil** such as a knife or **grater**. Ask an adult to help out.

Nuts!

This recipe includes nuts. Make sure to ask whether anyone you are serving has a nut allergy.

Kitchen Supplies

measuring cups

mini muffin tin

scoop

measuring spoons

mixing bowls

grater

cutting board

muffin tin

mixing spoon

paper towels

peeler

spatula

paper liners

whisk

11

Ingredients

Here are some of the
ingredients you will need:

whole wheat
flour

old-fashioned
oats

self-rising
flour

muesli

unsweetened
cocoa powder

all-purpose
flour

applesauce

eggs

bananas

blackberries

non-stick
cooking spray

blueberries

walnuts

zucchini

granola

vegetable
oil

carrots

apples

vanilla
extract

frozen
berries

Sweet Blueberry Muffins

MAKES 12 SERVINGS

Ingredients

¾ cup whole milk
¼ cup vegetable oil
2 eggs
1 teaspoon vanilla extract
¾ cup all-purpose flour
¾ cup whole wheat flour

2 teaspoons baking powder
¼ teaspoon salt
⅔ cup and 1 tablespoon white sugar
2 cups blueberries

Tools

paper liners
muffin tin
mixing bowls
measuring cups & spoons

whisk
mixing spoon
spatula
scoop

1 **Preheat** the oven to 375 degrees. Put paper liners in the muffin tin.

2 In a small mixing bowl, whisk together the milk, oil, eggs, and vanilla extract.

3 Put the flours, baking powder, salt, and ⅔ cup sugar in a large bowl. Stir.

4 Add the milk mixture to the flour mixture. Stir with a spatula. Add the blueberries. Stir lightly.

5 Divide the batter evenly between the muffin cups.

6 Sprinkle the remaining sugar on top of the muffins.

7 Bake 20 minutes or until golden brown. Let the muffins cool.

15

Cinnamon Banana Bites

MAKES 12 SERVINGS

Ingredients

non-stick cooking spray
2 medium bananas
2 eggs
⅔ cup brown sugar
½ cup plain yogurt
½ cup whole milk
1 cup unprocessed wheat bran
¼ cup vegetable oil

1 teaspoon vanilla extract
1 cup whole wheat flour
¾ cup all-purpose flour
1½ teaspoons baking powder
½ teaspoon baking soda
½ teaspoon cinnamon
¼ teaspoon salt

Tools

muffin tin
mixing bowls
fork
measuring cups & spoons

whisk
spatula
scoop

1   **Preheat** the oven to 400 degrees. Grease muffin tin with non-stick cooking spray.

2   Put the bananas in a small mixing bowl. Mash them with a fork.

3   In a medium bowl, whisk together the eggs and brown sugar. Stir in the bananas, yogurt, milk, wheat bran, oil, and vanilla extract.

4   In a large bowl, whisk together the flours, baking powder, baking soda, cinnamon, and salt. Add the banana mixture to the flour mixture. Stir with a spatula.

5   Divide the batter evenly between the muffin cups. Bake 25 minutes. Let the muffins cool.

Tasty Oat 'n' Raisin Surprise

MAKES 12 SERVINGS

Ingredients

non-stick cooking spray
¾ cup whole milk
½ cup applesauce
¾ cup raisins
1 egg
1 teaspoon vanilla extract
1 cup whole wheat flour

¾ cup rolled oats
⅓ cup brown sugar
3 teaspoons baking powder
½ teaspoon salt
1 teaspoon cinnamon
⅛ teaspoon ground cloves

Tools

muffin tin
mixing bowls
measuring cups & spoons

spatula
scoop

1   **Preheat** the oven to 400 degrees. Grease the muffin tin with non-stick cooking spray.

2   Put the milk, applesauce, raisins, egg, and vanilla extract in a small mixing bowl. Stir with a spatula.

3   Put the flour, oats, sugar, baking powder, salt, cinnamon, and ground cloves in a large bowl. Stir with a spatula.

4   Add the milk mixture to the flour mixture. Stir.

5   Divide the batter evenly between the muffin cups. Bake 15 minutes or until golden brown. Let the muffins cool.

Healthy Very Berry Muffins

Ingredients

½ cup all-purpose flour
¾ cup whole wheat flour
¾ cup old fashioned oats
2 teaspoons baking powder
½ teaspoon salt
⅓ cup brown sugar

1 egg
1 teaspoon vanilla extract
¾ cup whole milk
⅓ cup applesauce
2 cups frozen berries

Tools

paper liners
muffin tin
mixing bowls
measuring cups & spoons

whisk
small bowl
scoop

1   **Preheat** the oven to 400 degrees. Put paper liners in the muffin tin.

2   In a large mixing bowl, whisk together the flours, oats, baking powder, salt, and sugar.

3   In a small bowl, whisk together the egg, vanilla extract, milk, and applesauce.

4   Add the egg mixture to the flour mixture. Stir. Add the berries. Stir lightly.

5   Divide the batter evenly between the muffin cups. Bake 20 minutes. Let the muffins cool.

Zucchini Cocoa-Nut Nibbles

MAKES 12 SERVINGS

Ingredients

1 zucchini
1 egg
1 teaspoon vanilla extract
⅔ cup white sugar
⅓ cup vegetable oil
1¼ teaspoon baking soda

¼ teaspoon salt
1½ cups all-purpose flour
½ teaspoon cinnamon
1 tablespoon unsweetened
   cocoa powder
1 cup chopped walnuts

Tools

paper liners
muffin tin
grater
paper towel
mixing bowls

measuring cups & spoons
whisk
mixing spoon
scoop

1   **Preheat** the oven to 350 degrees. Put paper liners in the muffin tin.

2   Grate the zucchini onto a paper **towel**. Gently squeeze the towel around the zucchini to remove extra water. Put the zucchini in a 2-cup measuring cup. Press it into the cup. Stop when you have 1½ cups of zucchini.

3   In a medium mixing bowl, whisk together the egg and vanilla extract. Stir in the zucchini, sugar, and oil. Stir in the baking soda and salt.

4   Put the flour, cinnamon, and cocoa powder in a small bowl. Stir. Add the zucchini mixture to the flour mixture. Stir and then stir in the chopped walnuts.

5   Divide the batter evenly between the muffin cups. Bake 30 minutes. Let the muffins cool.

Supreme Gran-Apple Snack

MAKES 16 SERVINGS

Ingredients

non-stick cooking spray
5 medium apples
½ cup brown sugar
2 eggs
8 tablespoons unsalted butter,
    softened
2 teaspoons vanilla extract

1⅓ cups granola
2 cups whole wheat flour
1 teaspoon baking powder
½ teaspoon baking soda
1 teaspoon cinnamon
½ teaspoon nutmeg
½ teaspoon salt

Tools

2 muffin tins
apple peeler and corer
sharp knife
cutting board
mixing bowls

measuring cups & spoons
mixing spoon
whisk
scoop

1 **Preheat** the oven to 325 degrees. Grease the muffin tins with non-stick cooking spray.

2 Core and peel the apples. Cut them into thin slices. Dice all but 16 of the slices.

3 Put the brown sugar and 3½ cups diced apples in a large mixing bowl. Stir.

4 In a medium bowl, whisk together the eggs, butter, and vanilla extract. Add the egg mixture to the apple mixture. Stir in the granola.

5 In a small bowl, whisk together the flour, baking powder, baking soda, cinnamon, nutmeg, and salt. Slowly stir the flour mixture into the apple mixture.

6 Divide the batter evenly between 16 muffin cups. Fill the cups to the top. Place an apple slice on top of each filled cup. Bake 25 minutes. Let the muffins cool.

Super Muesli Muffins

MAKES 12 SERVINGS

Ingredients

1¾ cups self-rising flour
½ cup brown sugar
½ teaspoon nutmeg
1¾ cups muesli
½ cup plain yogurt

¼ cup whole milk
¼ cup vegetable oil
1 egg
½ cup blackberries

Tools

paper liners
muffin tin
mixing bowls
measuring cups & spoons

spatula
small bowl
scoop

1 **Preheat** the oven to 400 degrees. Put paper liners in the muffin tin.

2 Put the flour, sugar, nutmeg, and 1½ cups muesli in a large mixing bowl. Stir.

3 Put the yogurt, milk, oil, and egg in a small bowl Stir. Add the yogurt mixture to the flour mixture. Stir with a spatula. Add the blackberries. Stir lightly.

4 Fill the muffin cups two-thirds full of batter. Sprinkle the remaining muesli on top of the muffins. Bake 20 minutes or until golden brown. Let the muffins cool.

Tip: Try different fruits in this recipe. Apples, blueberries, and raspberries are great **options**!

Marvelous Morning Muffins

Ingredients

2 to 3 large carrots, peeled
1 apple, peeled and cored
2 cups whole wheat flour
1 cup brown sugar
2 teaspoons baking soda
2 teaspoons cinnamon
⅓ teaspoon salt
¼ cup flaked coconut

½ cup chopped walnuts
3 eggs
⅔ cup vegetable oil
2 teaspoons vanilla extract
¼ cup orange juice
½ cup raisins
¼ cup old fashioned oats

Tools

muffin tin
paper liners
apple peeler and corer
sharp knife
cutting board

grater
mixing bowls
measuring cups & spoons
mixing spoon
scoop

1. **Preheat** the oven to 375 degrees. Put paper liners in the muffin tin. Grate the carrots and apple.

2. Put the flour, sugar, baking soda, cinnamon, and salt in a large mixing bowl. Stir.

3. Stir in the grated apple, coconut, walnuts, and 2 cups grated carrots.

4. Put the eggs, oil, vanilla extract, and orange juice in a small bowl. Stir. Add the egg mixture to the flour mixture. Stir and then stir in the raisins.

5. Divide the batter evenly between the muffin cups. Sprinkle the oats on top of the muffins. Bake 25 minutes. Let the muffins cool.

Conclusion

Healthy muffins taste really good. They are also good for you. Making healthy muffins doesn't have to be hard. It can be easy and fun!

This book has tons of fun recipes to get you started. There's more to discover too. Check your local library for more muffin cookbooks. Or use your imagination and whip up your very own creations!

Make muffins for any occasion. Your friends and family will love tasting your freshly baked recipes. Become a muffin tin chef today!

Web Sites

To learn more about cool cooking, visit ABDO online at www.abdopublishing.com. Web sites about cool cooking are featured on our Book Links page. These links are monitored and updated to provide the most current information available.

Glossary

etch – to carve into something.

grater – a tool with rough-edged holes used to shred something into small pieces.

option – something you can choose.

permission – when a person in charge says it's okay to do something.

preheat – to heat an oven to a certain temperature before putting in the food.

supervision – the act of watching over or directing others.

towel – a cloth or paper used for cleaning or drying.

utensil – a tool used to prepare or eat food.

Index